Strange Borderlands

STRANGE BORDERLANDS

POEMS BY
Ben Berman

ABLE MUSE PRESS

Printed in the United States of America

Library of Congress Control Number: 2012946648

ISBN 978-1-927409-05-3

Cover image: *The Unnamed* by Petros of Harare, Zimbabwe

Cover & book design by Alexander Pepple

Able Muse Press is an imprint of *Able Muse:* A Review of Poetry, Prose & Art—at
www.ablemuse.com

Able Muse Press
467 Saratoga Avenue #602
San Jose, CA 95129

Acknowledgments

I am grateful to the editors of the following journals where many of these poems originally appeared, often in different versions.

Burnside Review: "Thirds," "Interruptions *(v)*."

Byline Magazine: "Playing Word Bingo. . . ."

Caveat Lector: "The Way."

Cimarron Review: "Interruptions *(iii, vi, viii)*."

Cutthroat Journal: "Obsessions," "Poet Attempts to Kill Chicken. . . ."

Dos Passos Review: "Beatings."

Drunken Boat: "Gallery Walk *(i, ii, iii, vi, vii)*."

Innisfree: "Crowded," "A Fragile Balance."

Knock: "Learning Shona."

Lucid Rhythms: "Parallel Parking," "Pluots," "Gallery Walk *(v)*."

Madison Review: "Passing Three Goats. . . ."

Pearl: "What You Can't Explain Once."

Pebble Lake Review: "Gallery Walk *(iv).*"

Powhatan Review: "Interruptions *(x).*"

Raintown Review: "On Detachment and Delicacies."

Salamander: "Nisha Questions My Need . . . ," "Interruptions *(ii).*"

Smartish Pace: "A Street Kid Fights. . . ."

Solstice Quarterly: "On Sex and Insects," "The Unseasoned," "Close to Closure."

South Loop Review: "Seven Pictures."

The Broken Plate: "Koan."

The Connecticut Review: "To the Safety of Goats."

The Cream City Review: "Endings."

The National Poetry Review: "Footing and the Solid Ground," "Quicksand."

The Worcester Review: "Moving On."

Unsplendid: "Good Grief."

Selected poems from this manuscript were awarded Poetry Fellowships from the Massachusetts Cultural Council and Somerville Cultural Council.

The poem "Interruptions *(vi)*" won the 2002 Erika Mumford Prize from The New England Poetry Club.

The poems "Learning Shona" and "Gallery Walk" received Honorable Mentions, respectively, in the 2008 and 2009 Erika Mumford Prize from The New England Poetry Club.

Distance and Intimacy: A Foreword

I'd been home a couple of years already but was still struggling with the blurred lines of where things end.

from "Gallery Walk, *ii*"

"Only connect," enjoined E.M. Forster, naming the fundamental artistic predicament created by the modern era, including in this not only the questions of fragmented form, but also the broken and disjointed sources of meaning itself. In the century since Forster wrote this, things continue to fall apart, within the self and beyond. Connection, however, is more easily said than done, and we still must turn to works of art to understand our troubles, and for ideas and images that offer new directions or better ways. There is an enduring felt dimension to our need for a sense of connection, coherence, and meaning. The poems in *Strange Borderlands,* Ben Berman's first book, speak anew to that need. They are in effect a report from borderlines between widely differing languages, cultures, and worldviews. These are poems that weigh, consider, and restore some flesh-and-blood meaning to the experience of multiculturalism, a word so overused it is often flattened out to a platitude or piety. But not in this book. Here we meet the all-too-human perplexities and genuine insights that sometimes rise out of the uneasy but simultaneous presence of truly differing ways of seeing, knowing, and feeling.

At the heart of this book is the poet's time spent as a Peace Corps volunteer in Zimbabwe, from 1998-2000. As the book begins, the poet is learning the local language and sharing the life of farmers in this deeply foreign culture. He works in the fields, eats the local food, helps dig graves, and in general joins in the local struggle against severe poverty. In the process he becomes filled with admiration for the energy, strength, and resilience of those he lives and works with. Making connections, however, is no simple task. We can see this in a poem from a sequence titled "Interruptions," where Berman and one of his Zimbabwean students are walking by a tree heavy with ripe fruit. The poet remarks that perhaps they could come back later, climb the tree, and pick some fruit. An innocent remark (in the many senses of the word innocent), it prompts a freighted and difficult dialogue. Tell me sir, says Edwin the Zimbabwean student to the young, white poet/teacher:

> *do you intend*
> *that we are like the monkeys?* Of course
> not, I say. That isn't what I meant,
> what I—*But isn't that why your people forced*
> *us to be Christians? You thought we were like*
> *the baboons. But now we are civilized.*
> That is not what I meant, I say. *You had bikes,*
> he says. *Bibles and guns. But also lies.*
> Edwin, it wasn't my people, I say,
> and besides shamwari, hazvisi
> what I meant. When I asked if we—*It's okay*
> he says, *Jesus is here. We are easy*
> *to forgive.*

Part of the beauty of this passage is in the delicate interplay of voices. What are the tones within these words? We, like the poet, perhaps are a little uncertain about how much irony colors Edwin's interruptions. Perhaps he is teasing, but perhaps not. Perhaps he is giving his teacher a little history lesson too. There seems a meaning beyond the ostensible occasion of this interchange, namely that whatever the Peace Corps worker is doing in Zimbabwe, he certainly won't be perpetuating the colonial hierarchies of the past. Let us also note that the poet here is learning Shona, one of the languages spoken in Zimbabwe. It turns out that we too must infer or learn a little bit of Shona in order to understand the poem. The reader too must stretch and work to grasp that "besides shamwari, hazvisi/ what I meant" is a Shona/English construction meaning "friend, that is not what I meant."

Learning the language of the other has wide-ranging metaphorical resonance. One might also say that in Zimbabwe Berman was learning a "life-language." This was no place for fakery, for inauthentic humanitarianism, or for hiding within oneself. There were elemental facts of life and death to face up to. Berman learns, for instance, that a goat will scream like a man when you kill him, whereas an ox will stare you down. And as Berman writes in "Learning Shona":

> . . . Zimbabwe means *The House*
> *of Stones* and I was getting grittier
> by the day, gritting my teeth
>
> and studying how to sharpen a knife
> on a slate, build a ramp and push
> a car out of the mud. Eventually
>
> I'd be fluent enough to sling a bird
> out of a tree, contain a fire, line
> a grave so water couldn't leak in.

Such fluency would, as with any language, come from immersion, practice, steady attentiveness, and need. Above all this was an experiential language. There was in these things he was learning, in effect, a heightened sense of the real, and perhaps across the cultural divide, the Zimbabweans were teaching the young aid worker more than he knew he was learning at the time.

The Peace Corps service, however, eventually had to end, and the volunteer had to come back home. Roughly the second half of *Strange Borderlands* focuses on the aftermath of the Peace Corps, the way those deeply formative experiences became absorbed and retained. Thus the book brings us inward, toward the poet's psychological landscape, and how it has been altered by his experience. Back home the solid ground has at least as much quicksand and "pitfalls" as Zimbabwe's collapsing riverbanks. Back home, for instance, the poet may be a teacher who has to discipline some tough students, or he may be parking a car on a busy street, but as he begins to look carefully at the familiar or quotidian, it too starts to feel like a foreign country with its own idiosyncratic norms and languages. As Berman writes in "Gallery Walk," a series of prose poems that conclude the book, a couple of years after Zimbabwe he is still "struggling with the blurred lines of where things end." The truth is in that "things" don't end as much as they bleed into each other, and for this book of poetry the past has become prologue, and the shifting present has become the reason why he must constantly reimagine and re-understand his past.

Or to put it more precisely, in Ben Berman's poems there is often a subliminal dialogue going on, one that shows this poet caught in the dynamic processes of negotiating difference. These poems interweave experiences with one another; they create overlays of dialogue and interchange; they show the mind stretching to gather unto itself different ways of being. Sometimes the overlays are temporal, sometimes emotional or intellectual. But whether it be in Berman's intense lyrical meditations about Zimbabwe or in his equally intense prose poems about the psychological aftermath of the Peace Corps, there is inevitably a flickering of new meaning, an insight, an ampler understanding. Even if the insight is only partial and ephemeral, it nonetheless has an authenticity because it has arisen from the frictions and abrasions of varying cultural paradigms. These are insights we can trust, and as a result we begin to feel just a bit more at home in that strange borderland where, as Ben Berman writes, "distance and intimacy collide."

—Fred Marchant

CONTENTS

III

IV

Strange Borderlands

I

Interruptions

i

A woman walks by singing to her baby,
Everything sadza, everyday sadza.
The name of the village, the school, the staple
food of the entire country, pots of
sadza everywhere. Even the first-born
of Marwizi is named Sadza. *It is life,*
my students tell me. *You cannot love women
without it. Do not worry. We'll find a wife
to feed you.* It all seems so simple until
I ask Marwizi how to make it. *Wait
for the first rains,* he says, smiling. *Then till
the land and plant the maize. But it's too late,
now. You will have to wait until next year.*
And the days go by so slowly. Two young
boys walk by holding hands. They stop to stare
at me, then continue walking. I bring
my radio into the living room.
Rhumba turns into world news, weather,
sports, Shona. Then Dolly Parton. Then drums.
Silence. More Rhumba. It never ends, never
connects.

ii

There's a logic to humor—its beat
pauses and flashes of surprise. But saying
hello, a morning run, the hair on my feet,
my glasses, garden, knees, nose, my staying
out of the sun—surely this can't be
that funny. I have a student named Funny.
A Lovemore, Learnmore, Trymore and Fanny.
A Godknows, Nomore, Bigboy and Munny.
Yet this isn't absurd here, this is normal,
nowhere as outrageous as when I sneeze—
then kids erupt. They fall to the ground and tell
me to do it again. They slap each other's knees.
Today, the headmaster announces—*you must
not sexually abuse the female students
anymore. But if it happens*, he tells us,
*just remember—it is proof if you get
any of them pregnant*. I look around
the room at all the other teachers and no
one is laughing. I'm tempted to stand
up and say, *especially me—you would know
my child*. But there are blank stares everywhere,
the sound logic sinking in. Tragedy,
the school clerk, pulls and twirls her braided hair.
She catches my stare and smiles back at me.

iii

Edwin and I are walking along a stream.
This tree, here, is called mashuku, he tells me.
It has very sweet fruit. Perhaps we can climb
it later, I say, and bring some down to eat.
Tell me sir, Edwin says, *do you intend
that we are like the monkeys?* Of course
not, I say. That isn't what I meant,
what I—*But isn't that why your people forced
us to be Christians? You thought we were like
the baboons. But now we are civilized.*
That's not what I meant, I say. *You had bikes,*
he says. *Bibles and guns. But also lies.*
Edwin, it wasn't my people, I say,
and besides shamwari, hazvisi
what I meant. When I asked if we—*It's okay,*
he says. *Jesus is here. We are easy
to forgive.*

iv

Makwezva joins me in the dirt.
We drive our hoes into the ground and tear
up the remaining roots of my first
pathetic harvest. *It is a new year,*
he says, *with good rains.* His son gathers dry grass.
We use some for compost, some for shading.
We add manure of chickens, goats, cows.
Sticks work as stakes, grass as rope. We're raking
seeds from plants from . . .

v

Two students visit my house
after football practice. They have an idea
for a business that they'd like to discuss.
Sit down, I say. *No, we should go to where*
we can make US dollars. They tell
me to bring my camera and prepare
some bread and jam for our travels. Noel
announces that he has jokes he'd like to share
but first he has a few questions about
America—*I have heard,* he begins,
that everyone has their own water spout.
And is it true that they eat dogs in
China? Before I respond, Tarisai
tells me, *Sir, this is what we wanted to show*
you. I look around, but I don't see
anything. He points at a young, half-clothed
boy—dirty and covered with flies. *Please, take*
a photo of this one, he says. *Send it*
to USA. Tell them to send money—save
African boy's life. They break into fits
of laughter, then begin trading high fives.
Send them my name, says Tarisai. *No, wait,*
first let us go and gather some more flies.
I take a picture of them laughing. *Take*
one of this half-built hut. Show them how poor
we are. Let's go, I say. We walk to Noel's
house and eat *sadza* with his grandmother,
stuff ourselves on roasted corn and boiled
nuts.

vi

I'm digging a grave with a shovel
that's too small. But I dig, dig until Marwizi
tells me I'm working too hard and helps
me up out of the ditch. *There will be
no more work,* he yells, *without proper beer.*
We get up, sit in the shade, the grave
halfway dug. An old woman falls to her
knees, begins pounding the ground. *We're not slaves
anymore,* a man says. I stare straight ahead
at the pile of bricks—my fourth funeral
in two weeks. I should know the songs for the dead
by now. *The beer will arrive soon or we'll
take the shovels home,* Marwizi says.
Makwezva takes my hand. *In our tradition,
you must pay the workers with beer,* he tells
me. *Chikanya is a devout Christian
and doesn't want beer at his home.* It's just
beer, I say. *Yes, just beer,* he says. *But also
our way of holding on to our past.*
Eventually the beer comes. And although
we still wait for our *sadza* and goat meat
we go back to work—get rid of the water
rising from the ground, pack the dirt in tight.
We seal the grave with bricks and mortar
then retreat to the shade with our buckets
of beer as Chikanya leads prayers for his son.

An older woman from the market
comes over and tries to sell us some
tomatoes. Marwizi tips his head
back, pours the home brew down his throat.
He dances as two boys walk by, covered
in blood, carrying the carcass of a goat.
I stand near the drummers, watch the body
being lowered, then dropped into the ground.
I should know these rhythms already,
should be used to overlapping sounds.

vii

The EU announced that elections weren't
free or fair. There was obstruction, violence,
propaganda and miscounts. They observed,
monitored, reported and have now left.
Most volunteers, too, have gone home already.
We will not be allowed to return
to our schools. *You can move to the city,*
they tell us, *if you want to stay and work.*
They're offering us a nice place to live—
a Dutch family will be away on
vacation—they have a maid, stove, a fridge.
They'll even pay us to take care of their dogs.

viii

I know we shouldn't have been laughing,
with their dog, dead, in middle of the road—
but the way Hilda exclaimed, *Ahh, that's heem!*
and the way I looked past the diving crows,
whistling, calling out, "Come here Cheetah!
Come get a cookie," whistling, until Steve
came back, collar in hand and said, *freedom
has never been so cruel.* We didn't want to leave
him there, where trucks continued to flatten
his remains—but what could we do with mangled
fur and piece of a paw? We tried to clean
what we could but everything was so tangled.
No one's laughing now, with Steve in the next
room assuring Hilda it was no one's
fault, no one will be fired. And me, perplexed
by this task of finding some comforting, some
explanatory words. *Dear Knottenbelts,
How is Canada? How is the weather
and food? Please make sure you tell
your cousins hello.* I'll let the letter
develop before I write, *Cheetah is dead
and the country is falling apart.*
I won't mention the crows or how Eric said,
may she rest in pieces. I won't explain that
a dog doesn't matter, so many people
dying these days. Nor will I quote Shona songs

or proverbs or point out how feeble
and stupid Cheetah really was. *Be strong,*
I'll write, *and happy for your other dog, for*
Lion, the new king of the backyard.
We're sure Lion is worthy to lead the hordes
of flies who worship him and his measly bark.

ix

In the middle of a meeting, the phone
(So they come here after losing their farms.)
rings. I hear it, but only look back when
(Why must we treat them like they are famous?)
a girl at the door says, *excuse me, there's*
(I hear they're only here until the term ends.)
a call for them, and amidst all the stares
(Watch. I bet they'll get to lead weekly sermon.)
we both get up and walk to the office phone.
(Look how they both go. They just don't fit in.)
Eric takes it and greets a dial tone
(I wish they would all go back to Britain.)
but says anyway—*Benny, it's for you*
(I hear they're quite good at speaking Shona.)
and so I try to greet the dial tone too.
(So what? Two have learned our language. So what?)

x

None of the boys are wearing any shoes.
They heat an old, used, plastic milk bag
over their fire then breathe in the hot glue.
The smallest of them takes one final drag
then stumbles through traffic towards me—
oblivious to cars and fearlessly high.
His pants and shirt are tattered, his feet
covered with sores. He takes my hand and tries
to sell me a wooden giraffe with three
legs. *Two hundred dollars,* he tells me. *Support
the arts.* That's art? I ask. *Fine,* he says, *fifty.*
Chibva, I say, and it's no longer sport
for either of us. *But, Baas,* he says. *Ndine
nzara. Please, Baas.* I take the giraffe
and buy him bread. He thanks me, walks away
to his friends, almost looks back as he laughs.

II

Endings

Last night, I dreamt
of returning to Zimbabwe.
Buses were running,
women were selling
tomatoes and I kept telling
Mavhundutsie he couldn't
be beating me in darts,
he was dead. And when
his wife brought me tea,
I refused because she, too,
was dead. Where was Dolly
Parton and the six-six mute?
Where were the overweight
ladies of the night? I remember
one monsoonish evening,
coming upon a shop that sold
soap and dried fish. The owner
offered me a blanket and corner
until the rains died down.
He brought out orange drink
and chunks of bread. *The ground
is wet,* he said. And I agreed.
Too wet, he continued. I agreed
again but didn't understand
what he meant until he dragged
a long, wooden box into the room.

My brother. And then again,
the ground is too wet.
And because I used to believe
it was the escalating hardships
that elevated us towards the sacred,
that the struggle, alone, validated
a voice, for a long time I thought
the story ended there—moving off
the blanket to lie on the cold floor,
wresting, rapturously, to sleep.
But the truth is I also woke up
the next morning and walked home.
And when I arrived, Maxwell
needed help with his homework
and Chikasha reminded me that
someone has to chop more wood.
And someone has to weed the field.

Learning Shona

At first, there were the obvious slips
of similarly spelled words—*penis* and
pumpkin leaves, Sunday and *foreskin.*

I learned *to pray* and *with ass* sound
almost exactly the same. And it wasn't
just language either, I'd see a man

suffering gum disease and write home
about the beautiful toothless smiles.
The same day I waved back to a group

of men, not knowing the opposition
had claimed the open-hand salute,
I confused a woman with a room,

announced, *excuse me, but I'd like
to enter you* as I tried to squeeze
by. The village idiot was a giant

mute—the one man in a hundred-mile
radius that I could outspeak—and even
he mocked me, would carve *UK*

into his forearm and point emphatically.
If words are, as Gary Snyder writes,
rocky sure-foot trails, I was learning

to uproot paths for artillery, pelt *iwe's*
at the children tugging me for sweets,
futseke wako's at the urchins high off hot

glue. But *Zimbabwe* means *The House*
of Stones and I was getting grittier
by the day, gritting my teeth

and studying how to sharpen a knife
on a slate, build a ramp and push
a car out of the mud. Eventually,

I'd be fluent enough to sling a bird
out of a tree, contain a fire, line
a grave so water couldn't leak in.

The Way

*When a man is tried, all the rungs and all holiness
are taken from him. Stripped of everything he has
attained, he stands face to face with God who is
putting him to the test.*

— Martin Buber

The kids and I sipped cokes until Zheke came
back with his cowboy hat pulled over
his forehead. I'd saved him *sadza* and *nyama*
and made sure he ate, hoping it would sober
him up before our drive home. We piled
into the back of his pickup truck and cruised
the dirt roads, cruised until his brakes failed
and we floated down a hill. God's grand test

wasn't whether we held on as we spun
off the road into a ditch, but came later
when we stopped to buy the kids roasted corn
and Zheke demanded I buy him a beer—
covered in mud, stripped of rungs and holiness,
I stood trembling—face to filthy face.

Passing Three Goats in a Field,
the Ropes around Their Necks
Tied to Tall Grass

It didn't matter that they were goats.
Everywhere I looked, back then, I saw death,
teasingly avoidable and unsheathed.
If they'd just eaten the grass that their ropes
were tied to, they'd have been free. But, like boats
tied to a harbor, they drifted and stretched
to eat the weeds in choking distance, their necks
now noosed because they did not dream or hope
for anything more than a lazy graze.
Hell, a herd boy could have flashed his knife
right in front of them and they'd have continued
chomping away, focused on the thin blades
of grass. And still, we go on, praising grassroots
and the sanctity of this short and sweet life.

Killing the Chicken
with a Dull Knife

Like a boy learning the cello, I bowed
his neck back and forth, praying that his skin
would nick soon. But with each stroke came errant
notes and straying squalls, some high-pitched staccato
squawks that sounded nothing like Concerto
in D Major. And like the boy who spends
hours practicing for his big performance
then stands in front of everyone and still chokes,

I, too, began choking—with my bare
hands—until his face slid off his throat.
And as I stared at his legs convulsing,
I thought, if there are *no ideas but in things,*
please, let this bloody *thing with feathers*
be ruin or flippancy—anything but *hope.*

Beatings

Brian used to beat his students because
otherwise they don't respect you
the same. Most beatings were harmless,
though. Latecomers would line up,
giggly and protesting, take two lashes
with open palms then shuffle off
to class. If they arrived without shoes
or wearing a ripped shirt, they'd receive
a third. No school fees, they'd spend
the morning untwisting barbs
out of a fence. I often circled
my classroom with a stick and hit
the desks when kids weren't paying
attention. Sometimes, I'd bring out
a sickle. *Just beat us,* they'd plead,
wading in the tall grass. Once, a student
turned in a Michael Jackson song
as his original creative-writing piece
and I made him read it aloud while his
classmates sang along. He hated me
ever after. When the soccer team protested
that their "sneaker funds" were misspent,
the headmaster spent morning assembly
publicly peeling large sticks as each
protester prepared to *Touch the President,*
which isn't nearly as metaphorical

as it sounds. The students, bent over
a desk, had to touch a picture of Mugabe
while the Headmaster caned their inner
thighs. Sometimes it got mean, though.
I remember Muchabaiwa, drunk,
slapping a young girl, a house servant,
across the face for walking along
the basketball court. I just stood there,
watching, the shame of silence burning
in my cheeks. I don't even remember
the girl's name. But Muchabaiwa's
dead now, his wife too, his kids
orphaned. And the school's closed
down—no more students lined
up and engaged in giggly protest,
as though it were all an orderly game,
palms open for punishments, beatings
they could count and count on to fade.

To the Safety of Goats

Kids used to throw rocks at my window and shout
　　Wakashata! then run
away to the safety of goats. A goat screams like a man when
　　you kill him. An ox

will stare you down. Tie him to a tree and take an axe to his neck
　　and he'll snort
and kick a leg, look you straight in the eye. One time, a rooster
　　fell down

the outhouse. You couldn't piss without hearing him cock and doodle
　　doo until Marwizi doused
him in kerosene and lit him on fire. For a month the entire compound
　　smelled like roast

chicken. That was before the kerosene ran low and the wood got wet
　　and we had to eat
dried goat meat and raw sweet potatoes for three days straight. You
　　could barely chew

goat dried, but at least it was meat. At least it wasn't the boiled lung
　　or intestine or cartilage
they'd serve when the ministry visited. During termite season,
　　we'd sit outside

with a candle and glass of water, pull their wings off, drown them,
  then fry them in a pan.
Kids would pack their pockets full and come to class with little
  v-shaped legs stuck

between their teeth. Better that, though, than dried maize and beans,
  farting and giggling
and blaming the girls. I ate grasshoppers on a dare, cockroaches to be
  polite and a rock off

a fruit stand only to find out later that it was meant for pregnant women.
  Mavhundutsie used
to tell me that I drank like a pregnant woman. He'd grab my collar and
  announce that

I was *ngochani,* threaten me until I opened my lips to the bucket of beer,
  until I could move
outside to the safety of *braii,* the familiar smell of searing meat, Makwezva
  asking me to pass the salt.

A Street Kid Fights to Keep
the Bread I Gave Him

It was half a loaf and probably stale.
Still, because of us, he had to wrestle

with yet another taste of injustice,
lick of might. From our privileged distance

we watched good intentions twist awry,
the merits of charity squirm away.

And despite our complicity, we watched
like blameless bystanders. We detached

ourselves, pointed out the cruel ironies—
not that poverty is somehow funny,

but the streets were paved with open sewers
and we survived, desperately, by humor.

We'd take each punch and produce a punch line:
Bread is life—but also, as the French say, *pain*.

Playing Word Bingo
at Meetings, the Week
Before They Sent Us Home

See, that is how we whimper for the small need of the hour
and forget the Glory of God is in Exile!
— Martin Buber

When someone complained about the bacon
being too greasy and how evacuation

would be better than another day of warm
beer, my friends and I waged a secret war

of words—enlisted *scuds* and *inaction plans,*
dwarves and *Goercke's mom.* And when someone

whimpered that they felt *locked up in this place,*
what delight we took in the small free space

in middle of our cards. We prayed for
getting the right words in the right order

and when we did—five in a row—we'd yell
Who stole the non-dairy creamer? Exile

came a week later, though it would be years
before that word appeared in my prayers.

Footing and the Solid Ground

Between swigs of beer, Muvhenge would speed
after the rabbits hopping through the headlights.
Holly began crossing herself vigorously, so I
yelled up, *shaz, usatiuraye.* Muvhenge laughed
and without looking over said, *why would I*
want to kill you? There's already one dead
body in the back. I said, *there's a dead body*
in the back? and then Holly repeated, *there's*
a dead body in the back? and then we both
realized that the bench we were sitting on
was a coffin. It was silent for a while
after that, other than the occasional swerve
and accompanying thud. Even the hills
had turned quiet, no signs of life anywhere
until we passed a bottle store and stopped
for one-one. I'd sipped mine halfway
and was declining advances from a heavy-
set woman when Muvhenge whistled
for us to leave. It was strange climbing back
into the car, having tasted the Pierian Spring.
Soon, the dirt road trailed off into a loose
landscape and we bouldered uphill over
mudstone and saplings. The car was
the only thing, that night, without shocks.
Jarring and slow going as it was, though,
at least we were staggering forward, unlike

when the path plateaued to cracked clay
and leaking wells and we found ourselves
mired in the muck. *Much of what happened
in Africa,* wrote Paul Theroux, *was not
tragedy but farce.* And here I was, stuck
in the mud with a cop, a corpse
and a born-again Christian. We searched
the area for slates or planks, anything
that might provide traction and grip.
We found stones, wedged them beneath
the wheels. Holly and I leaned on
the bumper as hard as we could, but we
were far from footing and the solid ground.
And the more we tried to push our way out,
the more we rocked ourselves deeper in.

Moving On

Every six months or so, Edwin writes
me a letter, lets me know who's passed
on and the latest cost of bread. This time
it's Benson, his younger brother Lovewell
and sixty-thousand dollars. *I am next
to nothing for money,* he writes, *and still*

*without work. But Brother, the Pentecostal
Church has arrived. They're teaching us the right
way to pray.* It's biblical—the disconnects
and catalogues, destruction juxtaposed
next to the austere and casual.
Procrastination is the thief of time,

Edwin writes, *and it has been high time
since you wrote back. Brother, are you still
alive? If so, send money for goats as well
as for beer*—the bill of burial rites.
But too often, these days, I think of my past
as a currency—rubbery chicken necks

and children named Godknows, boys who die next
to you on buses—I spend all my time
distancing myself, plundering my past
for sibylline truths and forget it's still
alive. Edwin's waiting for me to write
him back. He needs help paying for Lovewell's

funeral. *Back home, Edwin, all is well.*
Here is twenty dollars. I'll send more next
letter—it sounds so easy to write.
But *time wastes us,* William Matthews writes, *and time*
saves us and buys us. All we can do is steal
back from what squanders us, swirl the past

into the present, learn to trespass
even as we go light. Our rituals
grow rote, otherwise, prescribed and stale,
the mere expectations of what comes next.
Again, it is dawn. Again, it is time
to let go and hold on, time to write

back. *Please,* Edwin writes, *we need help. Lovewell*
and Benson have passed away. I am next. . . .
Angels, thieves of time, prepare to wrestle.

III

Koan

For years, I've grappled with one clapping hand,
grasped only the thud of a collapsing hand.

Still, it's how my inner life began.
My ear was struck by a clapping hand.

I sought soundless answers with an unsound mind,
I was drawn to the crash of a collapsing hand.

Master, I said, clarity comes in waves.
I expected the approval of a clapping hand.

But a *House of Stones* is a house of cards,
and I watched a country play its collapsing hand.

I clutched and clawed. I tried to hold on.
I waved goodbye with a clapping hand.

My life's grown riddled with such collisions:
the rising sounds of a collapsing hand.

Obsessions

Like Lorca's lobster dropping from the sky,
they hit me from behind then ran away.

And because it happened on a safe, well-lit
street, because nobody stole my wallet,

I found that mere forms and shapely answers
couldn't contain the chaos that ensued.

Now, years later, wandering past the snake
charmers and fortune tellers, beyond the smoke

and drums, I watch a man crack open
a sheep head with a hammer, scooping

out its brains and smiling all the while.
That same old tension—the casual

and the casualty. Again the hammer strikes.
Again the exchange of kisses on the cheek.

On Detachment and Delicacies

Even slaughter grows somewhat methodic—
you hold their heads to calm the spasmodic

fits of their feet, focus on precision,
how the right cut, like a good revision,

can produce a more deft and seamless
execution. And though later—when I'd press

my hands inside of them, wiggle their innards
free, then search for kidneys and gizzards—

of course I felt intimately involved, close
to life and death and viscerally engrossed,

but I was dumping hearts into a bucket
and wanted life to feel delicate,

wanted to handle each flimsy liver
with the fine alertness of a lover.

The Panther

after Rilke

Of course the panther circles in his cage,
his gait betraying a carnivorous rage,

but I've also witnessed the soft and tender
bellies of young impalas ripped, rended

open and ravished. Freedom is heartless.
Nothing's freer (the vulture knows) than a carcass.

Having returned from the veldt, I'm grateful
for my thousand bars and grated cell,

for the food on my plate (the confinest
dining in town!). Despite the rattling unrest,

restraint has helped me locate my elusive
blessings, helped transform me from captive

to captivated—pacing with partitioned
views and arresting flashes of vision.

A Fragile Balance

Because work has a way of stretching me thin
I've always thought of stretching as the ten-

minute warm-up before I run my laps—
push hard against a wall or collapse

into myself and attempt to touch
those faraway toes—I thought we stretched

to reach something, or, at most, to stave off
injury. But watching this woman lift

off the floor, spring into a fragile balance,
you'd think that stretching, itself, were the dance,

as she swivels and folds, streaming and flowing
from bend to arch to bow, her calf floating

effortlessly above the brass rail—
as though delicate were different from frail.

Crowded

Whenever I end up at Curtin's Roadside
Tavern, praising the dulling buzz of light

beer and talking to some woman about
the day's cool, jacket weather, how the clouds

seemed to threaten before they disappeared,
I begin thinking about all the weird

ways that I've almost died—the warm blood
that trickled down my thighs, the glass shards

on the ledge surely as sharp as the teeth
of the wild dogs circling beneath

me, as sharp as the focus on each step
when I grabbed the weak and bony grip

of a stumbling, drunken bus driver
and inched weightlessly across a river,

leaning on knees that hadn't locked so tight since
a scantily clad saddhu waved his tridents

in the air, then hurled a burning log
at my head—and I can feel my restless legs

burning and aching as they dangle
above the sticky floor, as my ankles bang

against the foot rail. And the more she leans
in close, the more I feel the space between

us, as though I've already crowded
too many stories into just one body.

What You Can't Explain Once

I drink to remember, not to forget,
so the world might feel vaguely
strange again. So many numbers
to keep track of these days,
so many buses on time,
you forget how to be thankful
for a dry shirt. The guy
next to me is telling some joke
about how to make a girl
hop around like an angry pirate.
He begins hopping, *hopping mad,*
someone says, and none of us
would be laughing so wildly
if it weren't three o'clock in the afternoon,
if the guy wasn't just back from Iraq.
Now it's my turn and I'm telling
some story about this midget I met back
in Africa, who used to hide under
the tables and goose the prostitutes
when they'd walk by. *I touched it,*
I touched it, he'd yell
as the women swatted him
with newspapers. The entire
place erupting with laughter
and AIDS. And another one about
this guy with one leg—you never

wanted to shake his hand because
he said *land mine* but your friends
joked *leper.* He used to sell porn
at the local market but found
there was more money in peddling
Jesus Fish to tourists. It's what
you can't explain once
you get back, what you think
you need a break from
until you find yourself waking up
early just to write about it,
or drinking late at night
or sometimes even in middle
of the afternoon, just to remember.

Quicksand

Even if we have a landscape
    to return to—not just some
setting peppered with baobabs

and thatch-roofed huts, but one
    that speaks to experience
itself—a dried-out river, say,

and the bank collapsing
    beneath our feet,
and even if we fell into

that groundless ground,
    found ourselves suspended
between a float and sink,

still,

we can't escape the unheroic
    rescue (friend, walking
stick) and how quickly

afterwards we forget
    our tentative measures,
sink into a sure-footed

rhythm, the pitfalls
  of solid ground
growing more dangerous

with every secure step.

Nisha Questions My Need
for a Dehydrator

In Africa, we called dried meat *biltong*—
thin strips of heavily salted goat that hung

from clotheslines. Not that I'm worried about
the upcoming dry season and drought,

but I love dried foods for their intense
concentration, their pockets of nuance,

their muscular notes of tone and tension.
Today, I received a letter from Edwin—

Mwarenga is dead. Marwizi is sick.
And here I am, concerned with domestic

pleasures. Nisha, I need this machine.
Sitting, watching distant and withering dreams

quietly implode . . . *find some way to revel,*
it reminds me, *in the reduced and shriveled.*

Parallel Parking

Poetry is the vehicle by which we hope,
nearly, to arrive at reality
— Donald Revell

Not that I've curbed my desire to roam
but I love these spaces where there's no room

for error—easing into a tight fit,
angling my way to alignment.

What seemed a crossroads, once, with adventures
far behind me and pedestrians, left turns

and rush-hour traffic everywhere else,
has unfolded—teeming with parallels,

paired up and pared down. Shifting into
reverse, the slight adjustments to center

ourselves—this, too, is the open road—
learning to navigate these narrow

streets—circling, pacing, searching for gaps,
watching the ordinary structures collapse.

Pluots

Every time the world grows stale with shelf
life and the perfectly bland, mealy flesh

of summer fruit, I find sweetness comes
in the least likely of places—half plum,

half apricot—heaped up in a pyramid
at this Chinese Market, a perfect hybrid

of possibility and better halves.
For years now, I've been trying to graft

the past onto the present. But not until
I wandered here, to this worldly and local

aisle, did I see some way to unify
the visions of the outer and inner eye,

to tear into this tightly fused fruit—
the best of two worlds, drippingly sweet.

IV

Seven Pictures

Riding Yemama

When a bus was late in Morocco, the word *retard* would flash on the terminal screen. Of the seven pictures that I took during my weeklong conference, three were of delayed bus notifications. The bus from Essaouira wasn't late, but it was called *Yemama*—and two more of the seven pictures were of that bus. One of Teresa and me on the stairs, entering *Yemama;* and another of us riding her—all the way to Casablanca. Now, when I come across these photos, I think of Susan Meisalas in *Pictures from a Revolution* asking, *how could that be? How could those be the photographs in which I'd risked so much?*

Shooting the Veiled Women

The viewfinder on Mike's camera swiveled so he could face a landscape while shooting close-ups of the women in burkas. I preferred a more direct approach, though neither of my final two pictures—of a shopkeeper cracking open a sheep head—came out. The images in the first one are so blurry that you can barely tell the hammer from the head. And in the second, every detail looks like background—all you see is some man doing something to some thing. Even with autofocus, I failed to balance how close you can get to your subject before the shapes begin to blend—and at what point, once you step back, the distance ruins the depth.

You say Collage, I say Collision

I didn't see Teresa get slapped. I'd been standing in line to buy bus tickets and by the time I dragged our bags down the stairs, the man who'd hit her had run away. A police officer pulled me aside, asked if I was in charge. *Not in charge,* I said. *We're just traveling together. We're teachers.* I looked over at Teresa sitting with her head in her hands and wished we were lovers. Or strangers. Anything but colleagues. Anything but travelers of those strange borderlands where distance and intimacy collide.

Slap Happy

Perspective, in photography, is when parallel lines converge towards a single point, and I wanted to lean across the aisle and tell Teresa that I, too, was once slapped in the face by a stranger. That this was what drew me to poetry—to broken narratives and lines that threaten to collapse underneath their own weight. I wanted to whisper this as Teresa heaved softly, her chin tucked into her neck. Instead, when we pulled over for a rest stop, I took her hand and found someone to take our picture on the stairs. She laughed wildly every time I asked the driver, in my broken French, *pardonnez moi, missour, but is Yemama a retard?*

Views from the Overlooking

The views of the High Atlas Mountains were as breathtaking as the brochure had promised. There was something too easy, though, about a bus ride to the overlook, to our guide's explanation that *great upheavals result in magnificent beauty.* Mike stood in one place and rotated, taking several shots in a row. He planned on stitching them together with software when we returned home. My camera stayed in my pocket. I didn't trust such a sweeping, expansive view—fragments that would line up, fit too neatly together.

Nuggets

A month later, back at school, Teresa and I are standing at opposite ends of the cafeteria when a freshman comes to me with ketchup in her hair. Some boys had been throwing chicken nuggets and one hit her in the head. Her eyes keep scanning the room and I can tell she's about to cry, but when I put my hand on her shoulder she shrugs away. I look over at Teresa, who's staring at the clock above me, and want to walk over there, ask how classes are going, what books she's reading, but I'm suddenly aware of all the flimsy nuggets fallen on the floor between us.

A Tale of Two Kitties

There were cats everywhere, and whenever I'd see a dead one—on my morning jog, say—I'd feel this small relief that it was someone else's driveway and I was merely passing by. Our last night in Essaouira, though, we returned to our apartment after *tagine* and red wine and found an abandoned balled-up litter of newborn kittens on our stairwell. I went to look for a shovel, but Teresa insisted that we heat a blanket, leave a saucer of milk in case the mother was still around. She picked the kittens up and held them in her hands. A few on the outside had already crusted over. Even then, I was hesitant to reach in, peel the dead off from those still gnawing.

The Unseasoned

When, as guests of honor in Vietnam,
we were served dog penis and the testicles
sat on our plates like Venn Diagrams

titled *Foods We Have in Common*—the circles
refusing to overlap—I made it half-
way to the head before I started feeling sick.

And when I finally put down my knife
and fork and all the hosts began to cheer,
I wondered if we'd been given the shaft

in more ways than one. The other teachers
kept coming over to buy me shots and pat
me on the back, take photos of the charred,

half-eaten penis sulking on my plate.
But it wasn't just the idea—the concept
that one man's pet is another man's pâté—

that was difficult to swallow—with no salt
anywhere in sight, the flavor was nearly
as tasteless as my colleagues' requests

for doggie bags. It was the ordinary,
then—the almost familiar taste on my tongue,
the way the mealy meat looked dinnerly

next to the rice and salad—that was so strange.
And as it became more and more plain
that this was not *exotic cuisine,* but singed

genitalia—undeniably penile—
even my determined attempts to
cover it with lettuce felt like pulling

the curtain back over Oz. Oh, Toto,
precious little dog, what did we do?

Thirds

The World

Ani and I were nineteen, trying to find ourselves by walking the earth. One late afternoon, lost in a failed shortcut, we sat on a clump of wet pine needles and shared our last orange, convinced we'd never make it back to the plywood beds we were renting for a dollar a day. We'd shivered through enough nights already to have shaken any belief in blessings and had begun clearing out patches of stinging nettles when a bearded man appeared among a flock of sheep, whistling and waving until we followed. He didn't speak. Only the occasional click or tapping of a rock with his crook. He led us to his tent where an old man sat in a loincloth spinning wool and smoking out of a hookah. Outside, the mountains offered their panoramic rewards. But inside, with our knees pressed against one another and flies covering our faces, the world had never felt so exposed.

The Door

Before Monty Hall revealed what was behind your door, he'd open one of the remaining two and display some shaggy, bell-noosed goat. Then came the big choice—switch doors or stick to your gut? Mathematicians have since professed that you're always better off switching, though, having owned both a car and a goat, I'm not sure the choice is clear. *Trust your obsessions,* Richard Hugo wrote, and how often I find myself returning to goats—stewed at funerals, strung out on clotheslines, their incessant bleating at night. The first time I helped kill one, our jackknife got caught in its neck. I still remember his eyes—their slow trembling—and his staccato screams for mercy until Steve jiggled the blade out of the bone and sliced his jugular. Warm blood spurting all over my arms. Monty, you opened so many doors for us, offered the otherworldliness of goats. But we were just kids, watching on our grandparents' couch, fooled by the beautiful woman who pouted at every last domesticated one of them. Monty, what could have been.

The Person

On that night I hitched a ride with a casket for a bench and ended up stuck in the mud, three men eventually appeared, rocked the car until the tires caught, then piled in the back. They began chanting and beating the bottom of a bucket. The quarters were too close, though, the vibrations too much, and I found myself as enamored with the tall grass glowing in the moonlight as I was disquieted by the dead man beneath me. We arrived and I had to help transfer the body into a small, homemade, wooden box—his leg rested in my hand, but it wasn't until I saw his kids that I felt the weight of death. I wanted immediacy, then. I wanted to sit down and console them. But they were off running in circles, playing tag. And besides, the others had already carried the empty police freezer back to the truck. And no one felt like staying for stiffened porridge and chunks of boiled goat.

Close to Closure

Say someone dies and leaves an envelope
buried in her underwear drawer, sealed
and carefully inscribed: to be opened

after my death. Imagine the usual
sentiments inside—regret and gratitude,
perhaps not a complete baring of the soul,

but a distinct voice, at least, an attitude
you'd recognize—until you reach the slight
slights and buried barbs—grievances that allude

to you. The last word's not the sole word to last—
still, it would be nice if the words inside
of letters were as mutable as the letters

inside of words—if we could set aside
those hurtful asides—or turn them into clauses—
watch how the intent would shift from incite

to insight if even if we weren't that close
slid to the beginning of the sentence—
the even if evened out in the closing.

Or what if we switched the tense—to not tense?
Oh, I know we can't change what words mean
but we do have means to negotiate distance—

measures to slow us down, marks that demand
separation—so that for a few seconds
we might step back and with a clear mind

observe our surroundings through a second
lens—all that guilt that had just enveloped
us, suddenly feeling sealed off, contained.

On Sex and Insects

i

Whenever Marwizi would put down his beer and start winking at those heavy-set ladies of the night, I'd try to slip him a condom before he slipped to the back of the bar. *No, Shaz,* he'd say. *I'm practically on fire.* The closest my loins ever came to fire was when parasitic snails burrowed through my feet, infiltrated my blood stream then settled in my bladder. It burned so bad to pee I thought I'd caught the clap. Still, on those days when it was too hot to leave the shade of my house, when the only entertainment was to sit in my kitchen and set up wars between termites and ants—intimacy, come evening, promised some relief from the aggressive boredom of the bush. Love under a mosquito net was awkward, but all that netting caving in on you—laced with insecticide—was the laciest thing around.

ii

It wasn't just boredom that got aggressive—I remember a man beating at my door, one night, begging me to pay dowry for some girl he'd knocked up who, having shamed her family, sat shivering beneath a blanket on her knees. And while you could calm a man with some cold hard cash, insects, come summer, were unrelenting. Fire ants would attack your toes as you walked to the borehole; piss bugs would leave trails of blisters along your chest while you slept. To protect ourselves from malaria, we took weekly doses of Mefloquine—a drug whose side effects included vivid, violent nightmares. For some reason that not even the nurses understood, those pills gave Maureen wet dreams. When the rains would die down and buses begin running again, we'd all head to town talking about the *three-month itch* and looking for a warm body. Except Maureen who, depressed that her wet season was over, would offer us the chance to sleep with her in exchange for our extra doses of Mefloquine.

Good Grief

The day after my great aunt was buried
and my house freed of relative strangers,
I snuck downstairs to watch some *late-night soirée.*

I was twelve, with dreams of being a ninja
or nudist and here, at last, was a movie
with both—large-breasted women in danger!

Later that week, as we sat shiva,
I recited the unadulterated
prayers. But every time I tried to grieve—

closed my eyes and clenched my jaw—naked
breasts would jiggle in fear. I didn't know
back then how to endure such braided

emotions, how to allow the undertow
to undergird. I remember the first time
one of my students died—this was years ago,

in Africa—I wanted to write home,
tell my brothers about the bucket-brewed
beer, the shovels and stones. But the kid's name

was Bigboy. *Bigboy?* It was too absurd
to include. I almost changed it to Robert
or Rumbidzai but I worried that would

cheapen the sanctity, as though getting bit
by a mosquito and dying days later
wasn't cheap enough already. But

Bigboy? Bigboy was a name for satire—
Alexander Portnoy thrusting forward
as the most infamous masturbator

of the twentieth century, his cored
apple calling out, *shove it in me Bigboy!*
giving a whole new meaning to soft-core

porn—and I feared that such feral joy
would undermine my romantic despair,
put the *fun* in funereal and destroy

the sympathy I craved. Not even Shakespeare,
who tried to separate his comedies
from his death-filled tragedies, is spared

such subversions. Right before Othello dies
upon his kiss, Lodovico proclaims,
Oh bloody period! And it does

not matter how many times you explain
that *period,* here, means *interval of time,*
a room of ninth graders will giggle in pain

as Othello gurgles on blood. There are some
stories, though, where the two are so interlocked
you can barely tell the dovetails from

the leapfrogs. For me it always comes back
to *Jermine*—a misspelling of Jermaine
tattooed on his right bicep. And though he jokes—

I'll just flex and tell the girls . . . 'jer mine—
this is permanent, curse and cursive
converged into an indelible design.

If only there weren't the preconceived
notions—we expect grief to come in stages
and when, instead, a stagecoach arrives

we climb clumsily in and try to triage
the tragi- from the comic. We hurry
this way or that, when all signs point to merge.

Gallery Walk

i

Of all the photos I brought back from Africa, I like this one best—the three of us reading the newspaper, two baby elephants right behind us. The President and his War Vets had invaded the farmlands like a *hair-lipped couple blowing on their fire,* which, for us, meant fifty cent safari rides and three dollar impala steaks all the way to Vic Falls. With nothing at stake, though, we grew tired of the game, tired of playing tourist to the proverbial life. The elephant in the room? No, it was the vervet monkeys who'd steal oranges from our packs, the baboons that chased a young boy who'd thrown rocks at them so they'd look up for the camera.

ii

At a gallery in Poughkeepsie, where "contemporary" translated into "formless," people were bumping their heads on floating pieces of driftwood. A young boy almost tripped onto a rug of pins. I'd been home a couple of years already but was still struggling with the blurred lines of where things end. In the middle of the room, a video played—a couple circling each other in the ring. The man was overweight, the woman shirtless and the theme music to Rocky made it seem like something momentous was about to happen. But the two just kept sparring, small jabs and lazy hooks while the woman's breasts jiggled about.

iii

I spent a morning, once, helping friends slaughter chickens on their farm and for the rest of the day saw gorged necks in every stick on the street, heard their pleading squawks in the worn-out pads of my brakes. *Because Pittsburgh is still tangled in him,* wrote Jack Gilbert, *he has a picture of God's head torn apart by jungle roots.* Finally, I thought, a haunting vision of my own. But it didn't last. By the next day, trees looked like trees again, chalk sounded like chalk. And if I hadn't dropped my keys, later that week, I probably would never have noticed the dead hatchling I'd been stepping over on my way to work—whose fluid-drained eyes and skeletal presence of wings had faded quickly among the gum drops and rubber marks to everyone but the occasional hovering fly.

iv

Because Kesey wrote when he was high, he thought of his writing as blazes—the trail back through the wild to what he had found. The blaze, for me, has always been the only way to tell a route from a root—my path to a hard-earned snack and view. No one marked the trees in Zimbabwe—not that it would have mattered—every turn led you deeper in. I had a student who used to look at paragraphs and see black squares on white rectangles. But walk through the woods with him and he'd notice paw prints and sharp turns, onions and death. He'd even learned to see what wasn't there midmorning no scurry of mice surely there must be an owl nearby or hawk in mid-lurk the sky as much a part of the earth as the dirt itself all absences ingrained.

v

It is no accident, wrote Heather McHugh, *that book, sentence and pen are the terms not only of artistic profession, but of penal containment.* Though the one night I spent in jail, the walls were hardly endowed with aesthetic engravings. The closest, I suppose, was amidst all the swastikas and cataloging of fags, one man wrote "I Heart the Cops." Then crossed out the heart. Nothing was framed, of course, other than me and my friends—locked up for sitting quietly on a stairwell while a policeman barked out orders then handcuffed us for "failing to disperse." The clink—similar to artistic endeavors? The only links I saw were the ones around my wrists. And the ill-fitted reminder that the getting in is much easier than the getting out.

vi

Three weeks before Zimbabwe's elections, two men tossed a Molotov cocktail through the window of an art gallery. For months the government had been impounding cars of photographers, banning musicians from radio—but this was a small family-owned shop featuring wire helicopters and ebony elephants, drawings of women drawing water from wells. That the gallery was located next door to the opposition's headquarters was *yet another sign of political incompetence,* laughed the Rastas at Unity Square. The next day they were selling ballot boxes in the shape of coffins, paintings of snakes eating other snakes' tails. *Buy something,* they must have been thinking, *while our canvases are still stronger than theirs.*

The man is running from one end of the screen to the next. He is galloping through snow and trudging through marshes, sauntering through living rooms and flapping his arms through federal buildings. Sometimes he sits on a couch, sips a beer, then gets up running again. Sometimes he somersaults naked. On the screen next to him, a man has brought a bow and arrow into a grocery store. He is hunting toilet paper and gathering tomato sauce. He arches an arrow through a frozen turkey—his craft as pointed as the tip of his shaft. Still, there is something about the man running and his dead-end flirting with the world—the way he continues on, flailing and unwavering.

Ben Berman grew up in Maine, served in the Peace Corps in Zimbabwe, and currently lives in the Boston area with his wife and daughter. He has received the Erika Mumford Prize from the New England Poetry Club and Artist Fellowships from the Massachusetts Cultural Council and Somerville Arts Council. *Strange Borderlands* is his first full-length collection.

OTHER BOOKS FROM ABLE MUSE PRESS

Michael Cantor, *Life in the Second Circle - Poems*

Catherine Chandler, *Lines of Flight - Poems*

Margaret Ann Griffiths, *Grasshopper - The Poetry of M A Griffiths*

April Lindner, *This Bed Our Bodies Shaped - Poems*

Alexander Pepple (Editor), *Able Muse Anthology*

Alexander Pepple (Editor), *Able Muse - a review of poetry, prose & art* (semiannual issues, Winter 2010 onward)

James Pollock, *Sailing to Babylon - Poems*

Aaron Poochigian, *The Cosmic Purr - Poems*

Hollis Seamon, *Corporeality - Stories*

Matthew Buckley Smith, *Dirge for an Imaginary World - Poems*

Wendy Videlock, *The Dark Gnu and Other Poems*

Wendy Videlock, *Nevertheless - Poems*

Richard Wakefield, *A Vertical Mile - Poems*

www.ablemusepress.com